BIOGRAPHY FROM
ANCIENT CIVILIZATIONS
LEGENDS, FOLKLORE, AND STORIES OF ANCIENT WORLDS

The Life and Times of

WILLIAM THE CONQUEROR

Mitchell Lane
PUBLISHERS

P.O. Box 196
Hockessin, Delaware 19707
www.mitchelllane.com

BIOGRAPHY FROM
ANCIENT CIVILIZATIONS
LEGENDS, FOLKLORE, AND STORIES OF ANCIENT WORLDS

TITLES IN THE SERIES

The Life and Times of

Alexander the Great	Joan of Arc
Archimedes	Julius Caesar
Aristotle	King Arthur
Augustus Caesar	Leif Eriksson
Buddha	Marco Polo
Catherine the Great	Moses
Charlemagne	Nero
Cicero	Nostradamus
Cleopatra	Pericles
Confucius	Plato
Constantine	Pythagoras
Erik the Red	Rameses the Great
Genghis Khan	Richard the Lionheart
Hammurabi	Socrates
Herodotus	Thucydides
Hippocrates	William the Conqueror
Homer	

BIOGRAPHY FROM
ANCIENT CIVILIZATIONS
LEGENDS, FOLKLORE, AND STORIES OF ANCIENT WORLDS

The Life and Times of

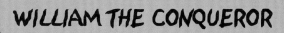

WILLIAM THE CONQUEROR

**Susan Sales Harkins
and William H. Harkins**

Mitchell Lane **PUBLISHERS**

Copyright © 2009 by Mitchell Lane Publishers, Inc. All rights reserved. No part of this book may be reproduced without written permission from the publisher. Printed and bound in the United States of America.

Printing   1   2   3   4   5   6   7   8   9

Library of Congress Cataloging-in-Publication Data
Harkins, Susan Sales.
 The life and times of William the Conqueror / by Susan Sales Harkins and William H. Harkins.
    p. cm. — (Biography from ancient civilizations)
 Includes bibliographical references and index.
 ISBN 978-1-58415-700-7 (library bound)
 1. William I, King of England, 1027 or 8–1087—Juvenile literature. 2. Great Britain— History—William I, 1066–1087—Juvenile literature. 3. Great Britain— Kings and rulers—Biography—Juvenile literature. 4. Nobility—France— Normandy—Biography—Juvenile literature. 5. Normans—Great Britain— Biography—Juvenile literature. I. Harkins, William H. II. Title.
 DA197.H37 2008
 942.02'1092—dc22
 [B]
                                                          2008020924

ABOUT THE AUTHORS: Susan and William Harkins live in Kentucky, where they enjoy writing together for children. Susan has written many books for adults and children. William is a history buff. In addition to writing, he is a member of the Air National Guard.

PUBLISHER'S NOTE: This story is based on the authors' extensive research, which they believe to be accurate. Documentation of such research is contained on page 46.
    The internet sites referenced herein were active as of the publication date. Due to the fleeting nature of some web sites, we cannot guarantee they will all be active when you are reading this book.
    To reflect current usage, we have chosen to use the secular era designations BCE ("before the common era") and CE ("of the common era") instead of the traditional designations BC ("before Christ") and AD (*anno Domini*, "in the year of the Lord").

CONTENTS

Chapter 1 Invasion! 7

             FYInfo*: Pevensey Bay
                 or Hastings? 11

Chapter 2 Before William................................13

             FYInfo: King Canute,
                 Emperor of the North 17

Chapter 3 William the Child............................19

             FYInfo: The Truce of God.............23

Chapter 4 William, Duke of Normandy.........25

             FYInfo: Harold's Brutal End........35

Chapter 5 William I, King of England...........37

             FYInfo: The Domesday Book........42

Chapter Notes...43

Chronology 44

Timeline in History 45

Further Reading...46

     For Young Adults..............................46

     Works Consulted...............................46

     On the Internet.................................46

Glossary 47

Index...48

*For Your Information

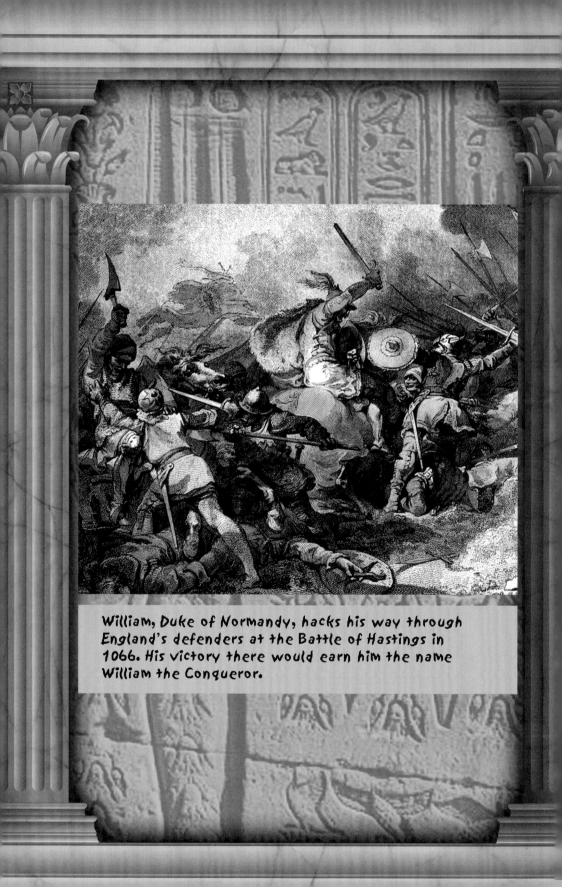

William, Duke of Normandy, hacks his way through England's defenders at the Battle of Hastings in 1066. His victory there would earn him the name William the Conqueror.

CHAPTER
ONE

INVASION!

On a late September morning in 1066, English peasants living near the southern coast turned from their tasks in fear. The deep blast of a Viking horn rumbled through every field and village. They knew the horn meant certain death to anyone caught by the invader, William, the Duke of Normandy. Many would choose death rather than serve the tyrant from across the channel who claimed the English throne as his own.

Frantic peasants hid in the nearby woods and watched the huge invasion fleet sail into the still water of Pevensey Bay. William was watching too, from the deck of his ship, *Mora*. One by one, his small boats landed, unopposed.

With no one to stop them, the invaders made themselves at home. First they took down the masts and sails of the ships and led their horses ashore. They used the masts and sails to build temporary forts. Knights rode out on a short scouting mission. Cooks lit fires and assembled roasting spits. William and his staff sat at a crescent-shaped table, while seaman unloaded provisions, and armorers, masons, and smiths set up makeshift shops.

From behind a hill, an English knight watched. Mounting his fastest horse, he rode toward London and King Harold. Soon, huge beacon fires were signaling the alarm throughout the southern villages—Normans were in England!

William wasted no time moving his army east to Hastings. If he occupied that port, he could control the inland roads to London. Small parties of William's knights terrorized the seaside. They burned villages to the ground—some were so devastated, the English never rebuilt them.[1]

Meanwhile, news of the southern invasion reached Harold. He had just secured an overwhelming victory over the king of Norway at Stamford Bridge in Yorkshire, but there was no time to celebrate. Immediately, he and his royal forces, the housecarls, began a hard march south. He had to reach London before William! (Historians don't know when Harold learned of William's landing. According to the Norman poet Wace, Harold heard the news before leaving Yorkshire.)

Soon, Robert Fitz Wymarc, an English landowner who claimed to be related to William, showed up at the Norman camp. He warned William to go home. Harold had just slaughtered over twenty thousand Norwegians in northern England and was marching south with a huge army. Defiant and confident, William boasted that he had sixty thousand men, but could defeat Harold with only ten thousand (which is closer to what he really had).

At that time, England had no professional army. Only the housecarls, the king's household troops, were a consistent force. The king depended upon his lords to provide soldiers. While Harold marched south to London, forces in the south gathered and waited. Harold summoned the northern earls Edwin and Morcar to join his forces in London.

The archers of England's King Harold overwhelmed King Harold of Norway, killing him with an arrow at the Battle of Stamford Bridge. The English king would march from there to his destiny at Hastings.

Men flowed into London from southern and eastern England. Edwin and Morcar never made it to London or the subsequent battle. Considering that their earldoms covered almost half of England, their absence was significant.

In Hastings, a monk spoke on Harold's behalf, asking William to return to Normandy. He acknowledged William's claim to the throne. However, King Edward, before he died, named Harold, the Earl of Wessex, his heir. Harold was the rightful king of England regardless of what the old king might have promised William years ago. William challenged Harold to single combat, which Harold angrily refused.

Two weeks after William landed, Harold marched his army south down the great road from London to Hastings. They stopped where the road left the forest and sloped downward. (At the time of the battle, the area had no name. Later it was named Senlac Hill.) Harold was still several miles from the Normans' seaside camp.[2]

That night, October 13, Harold camped and chose a good spot for battle. From the crest of the hill, he could see an advancing army. At the base of the hill, his men dug a deep ditch. His foot soldiers carried javelins and a two-handed battle-ax, which could split a head and kill a horse with a single blow. Men from the countryside carried farm tools. None of them wore armor.

Later that night, the English camp rang with song as the men drank instead of resting. In the Norman camp, William's half brother, Bishop Odo, led the men in prayer.

By 9:00 A.M. on October 14, 1066, Harold could see the Normans approaching from his hilltop camp. His men formed a semicircular wall of overlapped shields nearly half a mile long, with the strongest of his troops in the middle. They covered the slope of the hill that the Normans would have to climb. At the summit, Harold stood under his standard, a golden banner with the outline of a fighting man.

William's men split into three groups. On the left were the men of Brittany, Anjou, Maine, and Poitou. On the right were the French. Normans took the center. William carried only a mace. Around his neck, he wore a few of the relics on which Harold had made an oath to William a few years earlier.[3]

Close to William were Bishop Odo and his other half brother, Robert of Mortain. Also nearby flew the banner blessed by the pope. The Norman trumpets blared, and a single rider rode up the hill. Taillefer, a juggler and minstrel, had asked for the privilege to strike the first blow. He killed two Englishmen before others killed him, and the battle was on.

Norman bowmen showered the English with arrows. The infantry rushed the wall of English shields, but it held. When the Normans retreated down the hill, the English chased them. In the confusion, a rumor spread that William was dead. He rode straight into the fleeing men, threw back his helmet, and shouted, "Here am I. I live, and by God's favor will win. What are you running from? What madness is this?"[4] The men rallied, turned about, and slaughtered the English who had pursued them down the hill.

William ordered another volley of arrows. This time, the men shot them in a high arch instead of straight at the wall of shields. The arrows found their targets on the other side of the shield wall, piercing faces, bodies, arms, and legs. As the shield bearers dropped, the cavalry charged the protective wall, hurling lances into the unshielded masses behind it.

The English held their ground, but the assault took its toll. William wondered if they were tired and frustrated enough to break ranks again. Around 3:00 P.M., Normans trudged up the hill, taunted the shield bearers, then quickly retreated. The strategy worked. The English broke ranks and chased the Normans, leaving huge gaps in the shield wall.

At the bottom of the hill, the retreating Normans turned on the English. The Norman cavalry then rode in behind the Saxons and encircled the brave ones who had pursued them down the hill. Surrounded by Normans, the English stood back to back, and the Normans cut them down.

Up on the hill, the English tried to regroup behind the shrinking shield wall. Each time the Normans fired arrows into the air, the wall shrank. Late in the afternoon, a Norman arrow struck Harold in the head. Norman knights rushed in and finished off the English king.

By the end of the day, the matter of English succession was settled. The English dead littered the field and among them lay Harold. William, the Duke of Normandy, would be William I, King of England.

Pevensey Bay or Hastings?

What we know about the Norman invasion of England comes from several old manuscripts, all written nearly one hundred years after William landed. Wace's *Chronicles of the Norman Conquest* seems to be the most consistent, but there's no way to know how much of it is traditional story and how much is fact. Wace claimed that his father told him the stories. Most of our traditional stories come from Wace's manuscript.

Modern historians don't agree on many of the conquest stories. Perhaps the biggest mystery is where the Norman fleet landed. Traditional stories claim the fleet landed at Pevensey Bay. There, the Normans hastily built a wooden fort. Within a day or two, the whole army moved to Hastings to wait for battle. The question is: Did William land at Pevensey Bay or at Hastings? The truth is, we don't know.

If you consider the number of boats and the distance between the bay and Hastings, which is about six miles (fifteen kilometers), it is possible that the Normans landed along the beach all the way from Hastings to the bay. There were approximately seven hundred small boats. A peasant living near the bay would say the landing took place there, just as a knight living near Hastings might claim the fleet landed there—*if* the boats took the entire six miles of shore to land. If the small boats landed close together, side by side, they probably would have required less than three miles

Pevensey Castle was built as a Roman fort on Pevensey Bay around 340. The fort was abandoned at the time of William's landing.

(allowing twenty feet for the average boat width). It's important to note that the traditional stories do not suggest this, but it would explain the confusion about the fleet's original landing.

It is also possible that a small part of the fleet landed at the bay, found it unsatisfactory, and sent the rest of the fleet farther east. Some say the fleet landed at the bay and the army moved to Hastings in the next day or two. Others completely omit the landing at the bay. There is not enough evidence to solve this mystery.

For nearly forty years, Aethelred II battled Viking invaders. While the English monarchy struggled to maintain power, the Vikings repeatedly attacked England from a base in Normandy. After the Battle of Maldon in 991 CE (above), Aethelred offered to pay the invaders to leave England. They took the money but stayed. Aethelred's second wife, Emma, was the sister of Duke Richard II of Normandy. Their alliance made Aethelred so bold that he ordered the execution of all the Danish people (Vikings) living in England.

CHAPTER
TWO

BEFORE WILLIAM

It's difficult to think of England as anything other than Anglo-Saxon—descendants of the conquering tribes of Scandinavia and Germany—but it wasn't always so. In 55 BCE, Julius Caesar of Rome already occupied most of Europe when he crossed the English Channel. He discovered a wild and savage land of warring tribes. During those days, painted warriors hid in the forests, leaving its protection only to kill and plunder their enemies. These fierce ancient warriors were the first to repel the Roman army, but their victory was only temporary. Caesar returned, and his second attempt was successful.

The Romans changed the island. They lived well and built roads and forts, in which they gave refuge to the native Britons, who needed protection from the Picts and the Welsh. Britons preferred Roman rule to war with the savage Picts. For a few centuries, Britain was relatively peaceful and prosperous.

After the Visigoths sacked Rome in the fifth century CE, Rome withdrew from Britain and Europe. Without Roman soldiers to protect them, the Britons were defenseless. Once again, they were at the mercy of the Picts and the Welsh. Warlords replaced the Roman peace with civil war, using brutality and lawlessness to suppress the people.

Then England fell prey to another foreign invasion. Wave after wave of Jutes, Angles, Saxons, and Danes sailed across the North Sea and fought their way inland. Saxons were especially ruthless, killing everyone in their path. Not even women and children were spared. Caught between invading foreigners and homegrown Picts and Welsh, the Britons were surrounded by the fires of battle and death.

When these invaders weren't fighting the island's natives, they fought each other for dominance over the savage but fertile island. In time, the land of the Britons became the land of the Angles—Angleland, and later England.

A few centuries later, France also fought an invading force from the north. The Vikings were a hardy and daring breed. From their coastal villages in Scandinavia, these strong and brutal warriors crossed the North Sea to pillage villages along the coasts of England, Flanders, and France. Seeing Viking dragon ships approach, people dropped to their knees and prayed for deliverance from the Northmen. The stern, supporting a dragon's head, and the bow, with the tail, both reared high above the flat deck of the ship. Beneath the wide billowing sails sat the bearded Vikings with their wooden shields slung over their shoulders. The men slept on deck, as the long boats had small holds. No charts or maps showed them the way. They relied on the stars.

A Viking dragon ship

Once on shore, they blew their large ivory horns to announce their arrival. At the sound, everyone ran for their lives. Tenth-century France heard plenty of horns after the King of Norway, Harold Fairhair, banished Rolf Ragnvaldsson, called Rollo the Granger ("the Walker"). Rollo was an impressive Viking. He was so tall that he couldn't ride the small horses of his native land. On land, he walked.

Banishment was nothing but an adventure for a man like Rollo. He and a few other men, ready for adventure, made their way down the coast of Flanders, destroying coastal villages along the way. Eventually, they slipped into the Seine River and captured Rouen. From this hold, they continued their assault against other French territories. They took French wives and learned to speak French. When they finally wearied of war, Rollo met with the French king, Charles the Simple. By tradition, Rollo promised to serve the king, and the king gave Rollo his daughter in

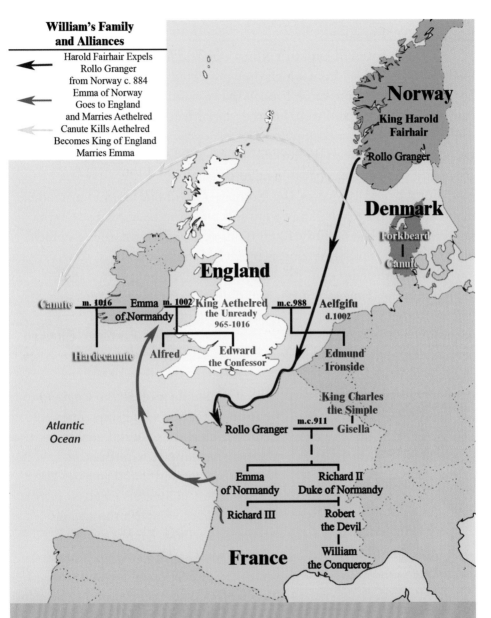

William's Family and Alliances

← Harold Fairhair Expels Rollo Granger from Norway c. 884

← Emma of Norway Goes to England and Marries Aethelred

← Canute Kills Aethelred Becomes King of England Marries Emma

Norway

King Harold Fairhair

Rollo Granger

Denmark

Forkbeard

Canute

England

Canute — m. 1016 — Emma of Normandy — m. 1002 — King Aethelred the Unready 965-1016 — m.c.988 — Aelfgifu d.1002

Hardecanute

Alfred

Edward the Confessor

Edmund Ironside

King Charles the Simple

Rollo Granger — m.c.911 — Gisella

Atlantic Ocean

Emma of Normandy

Richard II Duke of Normandy

Richard III

Robert the Devil

William the Conqueror

France

The Viking Rollo of Norway married the daughter of the king of France and became the first Duke of Normandy. His descendant, Emma of Normandy, would marry the English king Aethelred and bear him Edward the Confessor. Another of Rollo's descendants, William the Conqueror, would claim to be Edward's heir to the English throne.

marriage. Rollo's men converted to Christianity and Rollo became the first Duke of Normandy.

Rollo distributed land to Vikings who had fought by his side. They built towering castles from which they protected their new kingdom. Soon, the Vikings were more French than Scandinavian. Their lust for battle was still alive and well, but they faced battle clean-shaven. Their conical helmets had special metal pieces to protect their noses. Kite-shaped shields replaced their round Viking shields. They wore ring mail armor and wielded heavy two-handed swords.

For the next 125 years, the Normans fought one another instead of the neighboring French. They were still pirates at heart, and strength mattered more than nobility. Land translated to strength, so the nobles plundered one another, seizing as much land as possible.

Across the channel in England, Scandinavian invaders made a second claim on England. Aethelred the Unready sat on an unstable English throne, but relations between England and Normandy were good. Richard, Normandy's duke, even sent his sister Emma to England to marry Aethelred. The couple fled to Normandy with their three children in 1013.

Edward, son of Emma and Aethelred, spent most of his childhood in Normandy. Because of his piety, he became known as Edward the Confessor.

The couple returned to England to fight for Aethelred's kingship. They left behind their three children, including Edward, Aethelred's heir. Back in England, Aethelred found an early grave when Canute conquered England in 1016. Canute stole the English throne and Aethelred's widow, Emma.

Edward and his siblings remained under the protection of the Duke of Normandy.[1] When he returned to England as Edward the Confessor, he was more Norman than English.

King Canute, Emperor of the North

When King Svein I Forkbeard died on February 3, 1013 , the Danish army proclaimed his son, Canute of Denmark, king of England. At the time, Canute was in charge of much of the army. The witan, the members of the council who actually appointed the English king, opposed Canute. They recalled King Aethelred from Normandy, where he had been living in exile since his defeat in 1013. Canute quickly retreated to Denmark, where he assembled a huge fleet of around one thousand ships and ten thousand men.

The Danish invasion began at Wessex during the summer of 1015. For nearly a year, the Danish invaders fought northwest toward London, arriving in April of 1016. Aethelred died and Edmund Ironside became king. Edmund's army defeated Canute's in several small battles. Finally, Edmund and Canute met and worked out terms for peace. They divided the country between them. Edmund took Wessex and Canute took all the land north of the Thames River. When Edmund died later that year, Canute regained Edmund's land and became King of England.

He divided the country into four districts: Mercia, Northumbria, East Anglia, and Wessex. Military governors, or earls, kept the king's peace.

Canute married Aethelred's widow, Emma of Normandy. It is doubtful that this was a marriage of love. Most likely, it was political. Emma's sons, Edward and Alfred, under the protection of Duke Richard II of Normandy, still claimed the throne by blood. Marrying Emma left Edward and Alfred in the line of succession, should Emma not produce a son for Canute.

Most of the military problems Canute dealt with were on foreign soil. He also became the King of Norway in 1028. In his absence from Norway, many men tried to steal his throne. He died on November 12, 1035, still a young man—not quite forty. Before he died, Hardecanute (Canute's son) named Aethelred and Emma's son Edward as his heir. He would become known as Edward the Confessor.

Canute preparing to depart for England

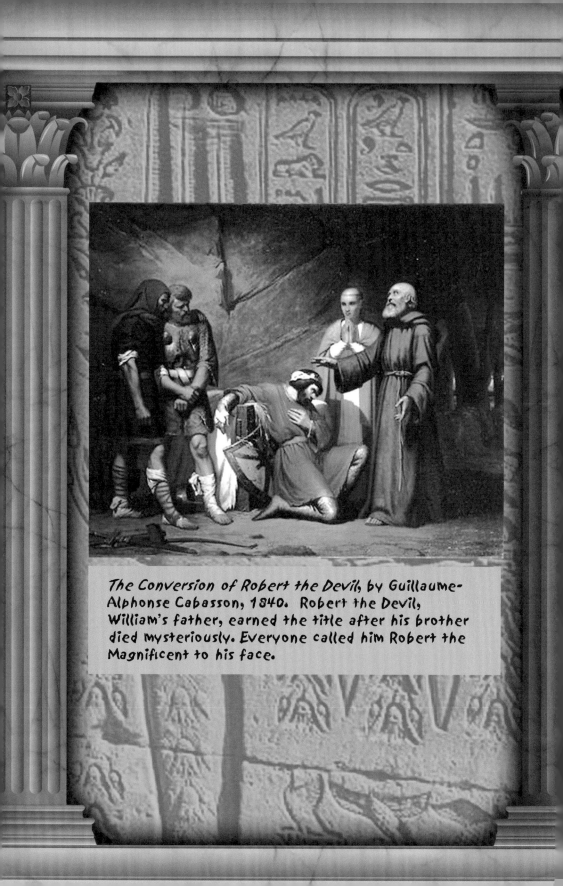

The Conversion of Robert the Devil, by Guillaume-Alphonse Cabasson, 1840. Robert the Devil, William's father, earned the title after his brother died mysteriously. Everyone called him Robert the Magnificent to his face.

CHAPTER
THREE

WILLIAM THE CHILD

The Duke of Normandy, Richard II, and his son, Robert the Devil, were direct descendants of Rollo the Granger. Robert's world wasn't all that different than Rollo's; only the enemies were different. By the end of the tenth century, Normandy was self-governing and no longer subject to the king of France. Other French territories, such as Flanders, Anjou, and Brittany, followed suit. The French king, Robert the Pious, ruled only a small area around Paris and Orleans.[1] The independent principalities began competing for power. They were constantly at war with one another and with the French king. Duke Richard II usually sided with King Robert.

Before Robert the Devil became duke, he controlled a district in southern Normandy known as the Hiesmois. His brother, Richard III, was Duke of Normandy at the time. Richard died under mysterious circumstances after ruling for just a year. Some historians believe Robert the Devil poisoned him.[2]

Traditionally, Robert met William's mother, Herleva (or Arlette), while in Falaise (in the Hiesmois). Her father, Fulbert (or Hubert), was a tanner, so she was not of noble birth. When Robert demanded her presence at the castle, Fulbert couldn't refuse. Herleva made only one request—she asked for an escort, which Robert sent, along with a horse to transport her. Surrounded by the escort, she left her father's house and rode to Robert's castle.

According to the poet Wace, on her first night in the castle, Herleva dreamed that a tree grew from her body—a tree so large that it shaded all of Normandy and England.[3] Of course, there's no way to know now if the poet invented the story to tell his tale, but her dream foretold her great son's birth.

Herleva stayed with Robert until William was born.[4] One traditional story tells that the newborn infant grasped the rushes covering the ground with both hands. The midwife saw this as an omen that the boy would be a king.[5]

William's parents weren't married, which wasn't unusual in Normandy. The Normans hadn't forsaken all of their Viking customs. At the time of William's birth, during the late part of 1027 or the early part of 1028, Robert, who was only about eighteen years old, had been Duke of Normandy for only a few months. He never married Herleva, or anyone else for that matter.

Robert sent William to live with his grandfather Fulbert, the tanner. The duke was generous to Herleva's family and made Fulbert a chamberlain. Herleva's brother took a post in Robert's household. Eventually, Herleva married Herluin de Conteville, a lord of moderate wealth and land. This union produced two sons, Odo and Robert.

Robert the Devil's reign was troubled by war and lawlessness. When Robert wasn't negotiating terms between warring nobles, he was defending Normandy's borders. Strife wasn't just Normandy's problem. It was rampant throughout Europe and England. In 1033, when King Henry I was driven from France by rebellion, he went to Robert for protection. During this time, Henry named William as Robert's lawful heir.[6] Meanwhile, Robert continued to protect Edward and Alfred, Aethelred's exiled sons, just as his grandfather had.

Early in 1035, Duke Robert passed his dukedom to his seven-year-old son, William. He was making a pilgrimage to Jerusalem, and he knew he might not return. However, Robert knew that his nobles would start fighting for his title as soon as he stepped across the Norman border. A dukedom with no duke was no dukedom at all. If infighting didn't destroy the country, a neighboring prince would conquer them.

It's not likely that Robert's nobles eagerly agreed to be ruled by a seven-year-old boy. In the end, each man placed his hands between those of Robert's son and swore loyalty to him.

Robert the Devil made the long journey to Jerusalem. On the way home, near the Hellespont, the strait that separates Greece and Asia Minor (modern-day Turkey), Robert died (July 2, 1035). As usual, poison was the suspected "disease."[7]

Within a few years, Alain of Brittany, the young William's chief guardian, was dead, also the victim of poison. Ralph of Wacey murdered William's next guardian, Count Gilbert of Eu. Instead of executing the murderer, the nobles named Ralph as William's tutor and captain of the young duke's army.[8]

William's third guardian, Osbern, also met a violent end. An assassin stabbed him while he slept, with William sleeping right next to him. Surely, had the assassin known, he would have also killed the young duke. His uncle (Herleva's brother) rescued the boy, and for a long while the family kept him hidden among the peasants.

By the time William was old enough to rule, Normandy was a country of individually owned fortresses, each at war with its neighbors.

The castle of Falaise, William's birthplace, was built on a rocky peninsula between two rivers. It was abandoned in 1617. Normans built similar castles throughout England after the invasion of 1066.

No one, not even nobles, was safe. What Normandy needed was a lord who could keep the nobles in line. They needed a leader, and they got William.

William emerged from childhood a powerful, healthy, intelligent, and unspoiled young man. At nineteen, he rode out at the head of his men to put down his first rebellion. At his side was his father's friend, Henry I (the king of France). William showed mercy to the rebel leaders. He confiscated their lands, and sent one into exile for a while. He sentenced only one, Grimbald of Plessis, to prison. Grimbald died there within a few days. William gave Grimbald's lands to his young half brother Odo.

Henry's help came with a price tag. Geoffrey Martel (the Hammer), the Count of Anjou, was expanding his borders into Brittany and Maine. Henry took up arms against the count and called on William for help. The young duke responded enthusiastically, leading an army that was larger than even Henry's.[9] Both Normandy and Anjou claimed the same duchy of Maine. The Normans claimed that Charles had given Maine to Rollo, but Maine's young duke was under the protection of Anjou.

William proved himself a worthy but brutal military leader. Near Alencon, a fort in Maine held by Anjou soldiers, William's men had to cross a bridge. Expecting William, the castle's defenders had hung hides and skins on the bridge. When they saw William approaching, they beat on leather hangings and shouted, "Hides! Hides of the tanner!"[10] Taunting William was a crucial mistake.

In the assault on the bridge, William's men took thirty-two prisoners. They cut off the prisoners' hands and feet and threw them over the wall. The town immediately surrendered.

There were more rebels. William Busac of Eu, and William's own uncle, Count William of Arques, ignored William's claim to the dukedom. Duke William's response was quick and brutal. He confiscated the lands of both troublemakers and sent Busac into exile. Count Arques chose to leave Normandy.

William was no longer a child in hiding. He was a force to be reckoned with, and Europe would never be the same.

The Truce of God

Robert the Devil's Normandy was a brutal and lawless land. Occasionally, the clergymen in the area would hold a council and invite the nearby nobles to reconcile differences in the hopes of protecting the peasants. The clergy would bring all the religious relics in the area, which might include bits of bones, vials of blood, clothing—anything that had come in contact with a saint—hoping to intimidate the nobles into behaving for a while. Usually, the nobles ignored the council.

Robert's efforts to keep the peace seem sincere, considering his recognition of the church's Truce of God. The terms made it illegal to fight between Wednesday and Monday. Breaking the truce was punished by thirty years of hard labor.

Pope John XV first proposed the truce in 928; it was applied in 1027 in Aquitaine. Originally, the truce prohibited fighting from Saturday evening to early Monday morning. The truce also recognized religious days.

Before the Truce of God, the church tried the Peace of God, which protected those who could not defend themselves, such as the peasants and the clergy. The proclamation was first decreed in Charroux, Aquitaine, in 989. It forbid knights and nobles from attacking or robbing a church; robbing peasants; or attacking, robbing, or seizing any clergyman who was not bearing arms. In 1123, excommunication became the punishment for breaking the peace. In time, the peace extended to protect children, virgins, widows, and merchants.

The Peace of God focused on protecting the church and the poor. The Truce of God extended the Peace of God by prohibiting violence in general on certain days. The truce spread quickly to Germany, Italy, Flanders, and Spain.

Catholic relics of St. John the Baptist. Before a decree in 1563 forbade the practice, relics were honored and venerated. Important agreements were made in the presence of relics to make the agreements more binding.

William was said to be of average height, but husky. He had a deep voice and was a good speaker. A strong man, William loved to be outdoors hunting or fighting. He wasn't considered graceful, but he was intelligent and shrewd.

CHAPTER
FOUR

WILLIAM, DUKE OF NORMANDY

At twenty-two, William was in control of his dukedom, although he was often at war. When he wasn't at war, he was hunting. It was around this time that he called upon a poor prior to advise him. Lanfranc seemed like an unlikely diplomatic and political adviser, but William chose well.

Lanfranc's first task was to find a bride for William, but not just any bride. William wanted Matilda of Flanders. She was related to most of the royal families of Europe. Her lineage traced back to Alfred the Great and Charlemagne. Henry, the king of France, was her uncle. Her father, Baldwin, was the Count of Flanders. She was even related to William, as they were both descendants of Rollo.[1]

William knew that Baldwin would be a strong ally. More important, all of Europe would recognize the birthright of Matilda's children.

At first, Matilda rejected William. By tradition, she was already in love with an English ambassador named Brihtric Meaw.[2] It didn't help that she found William beneath her: She said she'd rather enter a nunnery than marry the grandson of a tanner. She would have nothing to do with any "low-born adventurer who smelled of stable yards."[3]

According to legend, William rode to Flanders and beat Matilda for refusing his proposal. One story says he grabbed her outside of church and threw her to the ground. In another, he burst into her father's castle, found her chambers, and assaulted her. Whether either story is true, something changed her mind and she agreed to marry William. When asked why, she supposedly answered, "He must be a very bold man, else he would not have come here and beat me in my father's house. I will never marry any man but him."[4]

There's nothing beyond the creative verses of ancient stories to support this story. However, Matilda did eventually accept his proposal, but they did not marry and live happily ever after right away. The couple's happy union was marred when Pope Leo IX condemned the marriage because the two were cousins, as noted in an official brief: "It is forbidden to Baldwin, Count of Flanders, to give his daughter in marriage to William the Norman and he shall not receive her."[5]

They were very distant cousins—sixth or even more distant. Marriages between much closer cousins were common. Most likely, Leo was trying to help Henry of France, who had a right to be worried. A union between Normandy and Flanders would create one of the most powerful kingdoms in Europe. Lanfranc traveled to Rome to speak on William's behalf, while the couple postponed the wedding.

In 1051, the pining bachelor sailed across the channel to visit his cousin, Edward the Confessor, the King of England. There, William found a very Norman court. Remember, Edward grew up in Normandy, under the protection of William's grandfather, Duke Richard II. The court spoke the Norman language.[6] The head of the English church and the Bishop of London were both Normans. Norman earls were building Norman castles across the land.

It's likely that what interested William the most was learning that his cousin lived more like a monk than a king. Edward had no children, and it looked like he never would. Even more interesting was the lack of any other male heirs. There wasn't a single male with royal blood living in England at the time.[7]

William would later claim that Edward promised him the throne of England during his visit. Realistically, it wasn't up to Edward. He could name a successor, but the witan had to approve his choice. The witan was a council of wise and important men who chose England's king.

Regardless of what prompted the trip, William left England fully intending to be its next king. It could be said that the Norman conquest of England began in 1051 with William's trip.

Back in Normandy, William's thoughts returned to Matilda. In 1053, when the Normans took Leo IX captive, the couple hastily married.

Meanwhile, Lanfranc accomplished the nearly impossible in Rome. He convinced the new pope, Nicholas II, to forgive the couple and approve their marriage. Lanfranc made it clear that William would never give up Matilda. Worse, sending Matilda back to Flanders would most likely cause a war. The couple built two abbeys, Abbaye-aux-Hommes (Men's Abbey, dedicated to Saint Stephen) and Abbaye-aux-Dames (Women's Abbey, also called Holy Trinity), to atone for their sin.

William placed Abbaye-aux-Hommes in the care of his friend and adviser Lanfranc, who became the first abbot of the abbey. Consecrated in 1077, the abbey was dedicated to Saint Etienne (Stephen), the patron saint of Lanfranc's home of Pavia.

Henry I, the French king, showed his displeasure with the marriage by allying with an old enemy. He and Geoffrey Martel, the Count of Anjou, invaded Normandy in 1054, just a few months after William and Matilda married. Initially, William was powerless to do much, and Henry and Geoffrey were brutal, killing even children and old men. William needed time to assemble the Norman army.

Near Mortemer, Henry's army grew lazy when they met with no resistance. William, finding the French forces asleep and unguarded, set Mortemer on fire. Henry retreated to Paris. For reasons we don't know, William did not pursue him.

Henry and Geoffrey tried again in 1058. After a raid, the French army retreated. With the French army split on both sides of the Dives River, William attacked. Henry stood helplessly on the far bank and watched the Normans slaughter half his army. The French king settled the dispute by giving William the fortress of Tillières.

In 1060, William's father-in-law, Baldwin, became guardian of Henry I's seven-year-old son, Philip. When Henry and Geoffrey both died in 1060, Normandy was finally at peace. Thanks to William, Normandy was strong and prosperous. By 1064, William ruled Normandy, Maine, and part of Anjou.

About this time, Harold, the Earl of Wessex (England), took a sea voyage. Heavy winds shipwrecked him near Ponthieu, on the coast of France, where Count Guy lived. According to legend, Guy locked Harold up and demanded a ransom. Nothing suggests that Guy knew who Harold was, but it was clear that he was important.

Harold was the closest thing Edward had to an English heir and William knew it. Like William, Harold was a warrior with a good reputation as a politician. Edward was married to Harold's sister Edith. Harold's family prospered under Edward, and he and his brothers ruled much of England.

William paid Harold's ransom and gave Guy a nice manor in the bargain. Harold became William's guest in Normandy. In truth, Harold simply changed jailers.

During the visit, William treated Harold with respect, and Harold agreed to marry William and Matilda's daughter, Adeliza. He also agreed

Harold swore an oath to William under duress. He had no choice but to take the oath, surrounded by William's nobles. He didn't know, however, that William had tricked him into taking the oath over holy relics!

to send his sister Aelfgifu to Normandy, where William promised to find her a Norman noble as husband.

According to legend, William then called his council together and invited Harold. Earlier, William's men had gathered holy relics, including the bones and other body parts of saints, and placed them in a large chest, which they covered with a gold cloth. With the relics nearby and all his council present, William grasped his sword and asked Harold to confirm by oath the following:

✕ To help William, after Edward's death, secure the English throne.
✕ To marry William's daughter Adeliza.
✕ To send his sister Aelfgifu to be married to one of William's nobles.

No doubt, Harold was unprepared to refuse William—how could he? Raising his hand above the golden cloth, he swore by God to keep his agreement with the Duke of Normandy. Then William raised the cloth and exposed the relics.

Harold wasn't religious, but, like most men of that era, he was superstitious. To break an oath sworn over the bones of saints brought damnation. Soon after, William let Harold return to England.

There was more trouble brewing for Harold at home. His brother Tostig had lost his earldom, Northumbria, after a revolt over taxes and other abuses. Tostig turned to Harold for help, but Harold refused. Tostig wasn't a good ruler and Harold knew it. Later, Tostig would seek revenge on his brother for that decision.

Meanwhile, despite his promise to William, Harold married Ealdgyth (known as Edith Swan-neck), the sister of Northumbria's new

In the tenth and eleventh centuries, England and France were divided into earldoms ruled by kings. Power-hungry men from surrounding lands tried to conquer England. The English king had to be on his guard against Vikings from Norway and Denmark, Saxons from Saxony, the Picts from northern England, and the Welsh, from Wales.

England and Its Warring Neighbors (c. 1066)

1 Pevensey
2 Senlac Hill
3 Hastings

NORWAY
SCANDINAVIAN PENINSULA
North Sea
SCOTLAND
Northumbria (Yorkshire)
York
DENMARK
IRELAND
ENGLAND
Stamford Bridge
Mercia
Canterbury
Wales
East Anglia
Dover
Gloucester
Cornwall
Wessex
123
Flanders
SAXONY (Germany)
London
Romney
Normandy
Champagne
Brittany
FRANCE
Atlantic Ocean
Maine
Burgundy
Poitou
Aquitaine

earl, Morcar. Her brothers were two of the most powerful men in England, and Harold wanted their support. Morcar and his brother Edwin would be Harold's undoing.

Months later, a comet shimmered across the European skies. (Most likely, it was Halley's Comet.[8]) All of England saw the comet as an omen. Harold and Edward knew what they faced. William was sure to invade England after Edward died. A playwright couldn't have invented a better drama:

- ✕ Edward, the aging king of England, refused to name an heir.
- ✕ Harold, Earl of Wessex, had the best claim to the throne through his deeds, but wasn't a member of the royal family.
- ✕ William, Duke of Normandy, claimed the English throne by three venues: Edward promised him the throne years before; William was Edward's relative; William's claim went back all the way to Alfred the Great through his wife.
- ✕ Tostig, Harold's exiled brother, brooded in Flanders, waiting for an opportunity to seek revenge.

On January 5, 1066, Edward died without naming an heir. The fate of England was in the hands of the witan, who named Harold king.

Hearing the news in Normandy, William demanded that Harold honor his sacred oath. In response, Harold admitted that he had no power to keep his oath as the witan, and not he, chose the king. As for sending his sister to Normandy, she was dead. He was confident enough to ask William if he should send his sister's corpse.[9]

With Lanfranc's help, William took his case to Rome, where Pope Alexander II supported William. The English had always been a problem for the Catholic church. They were too independent. William would bring the English Christians closer to Rome.

Most of Europe's rulers also took William's side. Harold was the grandson of a cowherd, not a member of a royal family. By electing a commoner to the throne, the witan upset tradition.

When William turned to his own councillors for their support, they made a sensible but remarkably daring proposal for the times: "Those who take part in the work should also take part in the council."[10]

Agreeing, William summoned a larger council of landowners and military leaders.

This council produced at least one interesting twist, if the story is true. According to tradition, Tostig attended William's second council. William encouraged him to assemble ships and recruit sailors. Over the summer of 1066, Tostig used bribery and force to obtain men and supplies.

Eventually, William promised land and powerful positions on his court to anyone who fought for England. Volunteers from all over Europe answered the call. They came from Flanders, France, Maine, Anjou, Brittany, Aquitaine, Burgundy, and even Saxony (Germany). History refers to William's conquest as a Norman invasion, but in truth, it was a European invasion, led by Normans.

It took all summer to build William's fleet. William's family on his mother's side provided over 120 ships. Generous gifts of ships and knights also came from the clergy. Most of the ships were small open boats with a single mast and carried about forty men and a few horses.[11] Matilda secretly commissioned a special boat, the *Mora*, for William. Its flag bore William's arms: crouching lions.

*William's fleet, with **Mora** in the center, one of panels from the Bayeux Tapestry. The tapestry, created in the eleventh century, is in the Musee de la Tapisserie in Bayeux, France. It chronicles events leading up to William's rule of England. The beginning shows King Edward on the throne, two years before the Battle of Hastings. The last known panel shows the Normans chasing the English across the battlefield. Interestingly, the last panel is missing. Most likely, it shows William as King of England.*

Most early sources estimate that William sailed nearly twelve thousand men and thirty-six hundred horses across the channel in 696 boats. A few sources say the force was as large as sixty thousand, but given the limitations of the small boats, that seems unlikely. Most modern sources estimate his force was between seven thousand and ten thousand.

His men carried four types of weapons: lances, double-edged swords, bows and arrows, and the new crossbows. They wore iron-scaled conical helmets with nose guards. When William left Normandy, he carried a special banner and wore a ring sent by the pope. Entwined in the ring was a strand of Saint Peter's hair.

It was more difficult for Harold to amass and hold an army. There was no standing army in England. Harold had only his professional bodyguards, the housecarls, at his command. Anticipating an invasion, serfs, peasants, and farmers helped watch the southern coast of England that summer, but William never arrived. Finally, on September 8, 1066, Harold dismissed the local men, who were anxious to harvest their crops. Harold and his personal housecarls returned to London.

Unknown to Harold, William's fleet had waited a month in Normandy for favorable winds to carry them across the channel to England. Rough weather forced them to land along the French coast at Saint-Valéry-sur-Somme.

Meanwhile, Tostig was forging an alliance with the King of Norway, Harold Hardraade. Their combined forces of three hundred Norwegian dragon ships sailed across the North Sea. They ravaged the Yorkshire coast and then sailed into the Humber, which flowed between the two earldoms of Edwin and Morcar. Two miles from York, the mercenary forces of the two earls clashed with Tostig and the Norwegians at Stamford Bridge. It was over quickly. York surrendered to the Norwegian invaders, who settled in for a long celebration.

Harold marched north with his housecarls and caught the celebrators by surprise—most had shed their protective coats of mail. Before engaging in battle, Harold and Tostig met. Harold offered Tostig the earldom of Northumbria. Tostig asked Harold what he would give Norway's king. Harold is said to have replied: "I will give him six feet of English earth, or, since he is taller than other men, seven feet of earth, for a grave."[12]

William the Conqueror built St. Martin's Abbey, commonly called Battle Abbey, on Senlac Hill in Harold's honor. The outer walls are all that remain of the abbey's church. Other buildings on the site are used by Battle Abbey School. The church's altar allegedly stood on the spot where Harold died. A plaque now marks the spot.

The Norwegians formed a circular wall of overlapping shields. When the English forces dropped back, the Norwegians broke ranks to pursue them. Without their protective mail, the English cut the Northmen to shreds.[13]

Tostig should have taken his brother's offer, but he remained loyal to his alliance with the Norwegian king. Just as England's Harold promised, he gave Hardraade seven feet of English earth after an English arrow pieced the Viking king's throat. Tostig's fate was more gruesome. He was split nearly in two by a battle-ax. The survivors needed only twenty ships to return home.[14]

Back in France, William increased rations while the men waited for the right wind. According to tradition, William paraded the body and relics of Saint Valery before his men. In a solemn procession, the abbey's monks carried the relics through the camp. Soldiers fell to their knees and prayed as the body passed. Some made offerings by placing coins on the body. That night, September 26, the winds changed. A wild cheer rang out when the order to board the boats was finally sounded.

William's huge Norman force crossed the channel and found the southern coast of England undefended. After defeating Harold at the Battle of Hastings, William planted the pope's banner on English soil. Later, when Harold's body was found lying under his standard, William promised to build an abbey in Harold's honor.

Harold's Brutal End

William and Harold didn't meet in battle at Hastings. The duke did get close to Harold's brother, Gyrth—close enough to kill him. Gyrth aimed his spear at William, but struck and killed his horse (William was unhorsed three times that day). William then killed Gyrth with a lance.

After Harold fell to the ground from an arrow to the throat (or eye, according to some sources), four Norman knights finished the king. According to tradition, one of the knights cut off Harold's leg with his sword. William later expelled the knight from the army. Other sources claim they also cut off Harold's head and testicles. We don't know if this is true or not, but if William expelled a knight for chopping off the dead king's leg, one can only wonder how he would have punished the other knights. Most likely, only the one knight mutilated the king's body.

The next morning, Harold's mother, Gytha, offered Harold's weight in gold for her son's body. William refused. Harold, he felt, did not merit a Christian burial.[15] Modern sources suggest that William wanted to keep the body to honor him. We really don't know why William refused to return the body.

For a long time, no one could even find Harold's body. Finally, they asked Edith Swan-neck, Harold's common-law wife, who was pregnant at the time, to identify Harold's body by personal markings that even his mother had not known about.

William gave Harold's remains to William Malet, a friend of Harold's. He buried Harold's body, wrapped in a purple robe, at the Norman beach at Hastings. A mound of rocks marked the grave. The exact location of Harold's grave is now unknown.

Harold with an arrow in his eye, created by James Doyle, 1864

During William's coronation, officiated by the Archbishop of York, Norman soldiers stood watch outside. Fearing William was in danger, the soldiers set fire to buildings surrounding the church. The fire did not stop the coronation ceremony.

CHAPTER
FIVE

WILLIAM I, KING OF ENGLAND

Harold was dead and England needed a king—fast. The witan chose Edgar the Atheling ("prince"), a teenager born in Hungary and nephew to the late Edward the Confessor.

William retreated to his beach fortress, where fresh reinforcements were waiting. After five days with no word from London, he prepared to fight all of England. On the ride to Romney, his army destroyed everything in its path. Halfway to Dover, the army met a resident of the town, who handed over the keys to the castle. In return, William granted amnesty to Dover's citizens. The rest of England heard William's message: amnesty for those who submit, death to rebels. Hostages and gifts from Canterbury reached William before his army arrived at their gates. Other towns followed Canterbury's example.

London had no choice. They opened the city gates and let William in. A delegation of important men, including Edwin and Morcar, asked William to be their king.

William relaxed, but he didn't trust the Londoners. He built a wooden fort at a strategic point so that he could watch the city. This fort was gradually expanded and became the Tower of London.

William was crowned King of the English on Christmas Day, 1066, surrounded by important English nobles and Norman soldiers. As a matter of custom, those attending answered "Yea! Yea!" when asked if they accepted William as their king. The noise alarmed the Norman

The Bayeux Tapestry shows King Harold (right) dying from an arrow to his eye.

soldiers guarding the church. Thinking there was trouble, they set fire to the buildings around the church. The spectators ran outside, but the ceremony continued. The English clergy crowned William I before a small crowd in a smoke-filled sanctuary.

Shortly after the invasion, probably within the first ten years, the Normans commissioned a work of art to record William's conquest. Most modern historians believe Bishop Odo commissioned the storytelling tapestry. Today, we know this artwork as the Bayeux Tapestry. The French call it Queen Matilda's Tapestry, although there's nothing to suggest that she had anything to do with it. Today, scholars refer to this tapestry for details about the invasion. Interestingly, the end of the work depicting William's coronation is missing.

It was time for William to pay his followers, and he did so with confiscated English land. These conquering Normans became England's new aristocracy.

As promised, William divided England into small feudal fiefs—estates where the lord was loyal to the king—which he distributed to the Normans. Of course, this upset the old English families, who were out of favor, out of power, and suddenly out of their homes. Naturally, there were revolts. William was king in London, but England was larger than just London.

William ordered the newly established Norman lords to build castles. At first, these castles were small wooden forts, which the Normans replaced with elaborate stone castles. From these castles, Norman lords kept the peace. By introducing the Norman feudal system to England,

William was the first to unite the whole of England under a central government.

By uniting the country, he put an end to the constant squabbling and border disputes. To his credit, he left local sheriffs in place. Allowing the English to maintain their system of law and order within their small communities was an innovative decision. Once it was clear that William's new government wasn't going to change their everyday lives, most Englishmen submitted to their new king. However, William filled vacated posts with Normans or men of any other nationality than English.

By 1068, England was quiet enough that he sent for Matilda. On May 11, 1068, she was crowned the first queen of England. Before Matilda, a king's wife was just that: the king's wife.

Agatha, the royal couple's daughter, also came to England. Edwin, the same earl who betrayed Harold at the Battle of Hastings, asked for her hand in marriage. When William put him off, Edwin retreated to the north and stirred up a revolt, which William quickly put down. As a result, William possessed York, the most important town in England after London.

Significant rebels fled to Scotland. In fact, so many men from the north defected to Scotland that, to avoid confrontation, Malcolm of Scotland sent word to William that he wanted to discuss peace terms.

Fleeing English rebels sought protection from William in Scotland. Malcolm III accommodated many of them at Edinburgh Castle (right). Malcolm raided northern England so often that William finally marched into Scotland, which quickly submitted to William.

Near the end of 1068, Matilda gave birth to a son. They named him Henry. As the son of the reigning king, Henry was the heir to the English throne. (In 1100, he would be crowned King Henry I and rule England until his death in 1135.)

William's peace was troubled. He had to subdue York three times. Harold's sons attacked from Ireland. Even the Danes tried to take England. William was relentless and brutal in his responses. His army ravaged Yorkshire (Northumbria). Those they didn't kill starved to death in the aftermath. Twenty years later, the land was still wilderness—having been totally abandoned and neglected.[1]

In 1070, Edwin finally lost his head, literally, in the last meaningful revolt of the English people against William I. Morcar, his brother, was among the many prisoners taken. William sent him to Normandy, where he spent the rest of his life in prison. Other rebels forfeited limbs or eyes. Some spent the remainder of their lives in Norman dungeons. The conquering was over, and William was finally free to reign as England's king.

That same year, William rewarded his faithful adviser Lanfranc by making him archbishop of Canterbury. England can thank Lanfranc for its many cathedrals. He also made the church very land-wealthy.[2]

Also that year, Malcolm of Scotland broke his peace with William and plundered lands along the border. In 1071, William led an expedition into Scotland. Malcolm put up no resistance and submitted quickly to William. Without a single battle, William was king of both England and Scotland.[3]

In 1085, William commissioned the Domesday Book, which recorded land holdings among the Norman barons. This book is famous for being the first document used as a legally binding contract. The book also contained England's first census.

William returned to Normandy in 1087. After burning Mantes, a town near Paris, he was thrown from his horse. Some sources say he burned as well; others claim that he suffered internal injuries when the panicked horse threw him against the saddle's pommel, which burst his intestines; and others say he was dehorsed by his son Robert during Robert's rebellion. It took him five weeks to die. At his death on September 9, 1087, he was about sixty years old. His body was enshrined

An 1832 engraving shows Robert of Normandy (William's son) dehorsing William the Conqueror in a battle during Robert's Rebellion. It is one of many scenarios of William's death.

at Saint Stephen's, the abbey he had built in Caen, Normandy. The abbey still stands, but without the king's remains. Huguenots (French Protestants) scattered his bones in 1562. French Revolutionaries further desecrated the site in 1793.

William's conquest is one of the most important events in English history. Thanks to William, England was tied to France, Western Europe, and the Scandinavian countries. He was the first to distribute land in squared-off parcels and the first to use written documents as legally binding contracts.

While King of England, William enacted new laws, but he kept the existing central government. He developed a system of military defense based on land tenure, giving rise to the feudal system in England. William was the only English king to make himself king of all England by conquest.[4] Perhaps more importantly, England hasn't been successfully invaded since. William united England and left it strong enough to compete as humankind crawled out of the Dark Ages and into a modern world.

The Domesday Book

Celebrating Christmas at Gloucester in 1085, William asked for a survey of all the counties in southern England. It was an enormous undertaking for the time. Within each county, each landowner's holdings are described, including estates and manors; the landowner's English predecessor (preinvasion); the tax assessment; the property's value; and the number of peasants and other assets, such as livestock. The surveys were collected in the Domesday Book.

We don't know William's motive for wanting the records, but it was a useful administrative tool. As such, his representatives used it to collect taxes and determine jurors. It is possible that William simply wanted to know just how wealthy England was. It seems just as likely that he hoped the survey would resolve property disputes. Politically, the survey legitimized, to an extent, the invasion.

Around mid-1086, William received the finished survey in a regal ceremony known as the Salisbury Oath, during which all of his vassals came together at one time to swear an oath of allegiance to him. Before leaving for Normandy, William packed the survey away in the royal treasury, which is an indication of how important the Normans considered the information.

The original manuscripts are at the Public Record Office in London. There are actually two manuscripts: Little Domesday and Great Domesday. Little Domesday appears to be a rough draft of the final document, Great Domesday.

The Domesday Book, England's first known census, is housed in a specially made chest at The National Archives in Kew, London.

CHAPTER NOTES

Chapter One. Invasion!

1. Michael Wood, *In Search of the Dark Ages* (New York: Facts on File Publications, 1987), p. 220.

2. George Slocombe, *William the Conqueror* (New York: G. P. Putnam's Sons, 1961), p. 146.

3. Phillips Russell, *William the Conqueror* (New York: Charles Scribner's Sons, 1933), p. 152.

4. Ibid., p. 154.

Chapter Two. Before William

1. David Bates, *William the Conqueror* (London: George Phillip Ltd., 1989), p. 10.

Chapter Three. William the Child

1. David Bates, *William the Conqueror* (London: George Phillip Ltd., 1989), p. 8.

2. Ibid., p. 23.

3. Phillips Russell, *William the Conqueror* (New York: Charles Scribner's Sons, 1933), p. 20.

4. Ibid., p. 19.

5. Ibid., p. 20.

6. Bates, p. 24.

7. Russell, p. 24.

8. Ibid., p. 25.

9. Ibid., p. 43.

10. Ibid., p. 46.

Chapter Four.
William, Duke of Normandy

1. Phillips Russell, *William the Conqueror* (New York: Charles Scribner's Sons, 1933), p. 55.

2. Ibid., p. 3.

3. Ibid., p. 56.

4. Ibid., p. 64.

5. Ibid., p. 57.

6. Ibid., p. 60.

7. Ibid., p. 61.

8. Ibid., p. 98.

9. Ibid., p. 102.

10. Ibid., p. 110.

11. Ibid., p. 125.

12. Michael Wood, *In Search of the Dark Ages* (New York: Facts on File Publications, 1987), p. 218.

13. Russell, p. 121.

14. Nigel Blundell and Kate Farrington, *Ancient England* (Edison, New Jersey: Chartwell Books, Inc., 1996), p. 60.

15. George Slocombe, *William the Conqueror* (New York: G. P. Putnam's Sons, 1959), p. 156.

Chapter Five.
William I, King of England

1. Phillips Russell, *William the Conqueror* (New York: Charles Scribner's Sons, 1933), p. 213.

2. Ibid., p. 223.

3. Ibid., p. 237.

4. George Slocombe, *William the Conqueror* (New York: G. P. Putnam's Sons, 1959), p. 262.

**1027
or 1028**   William is born in Falaise, Normandy, to Duke Robert I of Normandy and Herleva (also known as Arlette).

1035   William becomes Duke of Normandy at age seven. His father dies while on pilgrimage to Jerusalem.

1051   William visits Edward the Confessor in England. He claims Edward promised him the throne.

1053   William marries Matilda of Flanders.

1054   Geoffrey Martel and Henry I invade Normandy.

1058   Geoffrey Martel and Henry I invade Normandy again.

1060   Goeffrey Martel and Henry I die.

1062   William annexes Maine.

1066   Edward the Confessor dies without naming an heir, and Harold of Wessex is crowned king. William spends the summer building a fleet and gathering his army.

September 6   Harold releases southern watch, leaving the southern coast of England vulnerable.

September 25   Battle of Stamford Bridge; Harold Hardraade and Tostig die.

September 26   William's fleet heads for England, arriving two days later.

October 13   Harold's army camps at Senlac Hill.

October 14   William defeats Harold at the Battle of Hastings.

December 25   William is crowned William I, King of England.

1068   Matilda is crowned Queen of England on May 11. She gives birth to Henry—who will inherit the English throne.

1070   Edwin is beheaded, and Morcar is sent to live out his life in a Norman prison.

1071   William rules Scotland after Malcolm III pays William homage.

1073   William conquers Maine.

1085   William commissions the Domesday Book to record land acquisitions and assets.

1087   William returns to Normandy. He goes to war with Philip I of France. His son Robert stages a rebellion. William dies from injuries on September 9, and his land is divided between Robert Curthose and another son, William Rufus.

TIMELINE IN HISTORY

800–814	Charlemagne rules the Holy Roman Empire.
c. 800	Vikings raid Europe.
844	Vikings conquer islands off the coast of France.
851	Vikings raid England.
911	King Charles III gives Normandy to Rollo.
989	Church introduces Peace of God.
996–1031	Robert the Pious reigns over France.
1014	King Svein dies, and the Danish army proclaims Canute its king. Aethelred the Unready and Emma of Normandy seek protection in Normandy.
1015	Danes invade London.
1016	Danish army arrives in London. Canute of Denmark conquers England.
1016–1030	Peace of God and Truce of God legislation are passed throughout Europe.
1027	Robert the Devil becomes Duke of Normandy. The Church introduces Truce of God in Aquitaine.
1035	King Canute dies on November 12.
1046	Harold Hardraade becomes king of Norway.
1066	Normans conquer southern Italy.
1091	Normans conquer Sicily.
1097	The Knights Crusade (First Crusade) begins.
1099	Christian Crusaders capture Jerusalem.
1100	William I's son Henry is crowned King of England.
1144	Geoffrey V Plantagenet of Anjou, son of Henry I, takes Normandy.
1157	Richard the Lionheart is born to Henry II and Eleanor of Aquitaine.

FURTHER READING

For Young Adults

Bridgeford, Andrew. *1066: The Hidden History in the Bayeux Tapestry.* New York: Walker & Company, 2006.

Davis, Barbara J. *Conquering England: The Battle of Hastings.* Mankato, Minnesota: Capstone Press, 2008.

Graham-Campbell, James. *Viking World.* London: Frances Lincoln, 2006.

Hilliam, Paul. *William the Conqueror: The First Norman King of England.* New York: Rosen Publishing Group, 2004.

McGowen, Tom. *William the Conqueror: Last Invader of England.* Berkeley Heights: Enslow Publishing, Inc., 2006.

Tames, Richard. *Discovery Plus: Knights and Battles.* Berkley, California: Silver Dolphin, 2001.

Tappan, Eva March. *In the Days of William the Conqueror.* Chapel Hill, North Carolina: Yesterday's Classics, 2006.

Works Consulted

Bates, David. *William the Conqueror.* London: George Phillip Ltd., 1989.

Blundell, Nigel, and Kate Farrington. *Ancient England.* Edison, New Jersey: Chartwell Books, Inc., 1996.

Clanchy, M. T. *England and Its Rulers, Second Edition.* Oxford, England: Blackwell Publishers, 1998.

Edge, David, and John Miles Paddock. *Arms & Armor of the Medieval Knight: An Illustrated History of Weaponry in the Middle Ages.* New York: Crescent Books, 1988.

Haskins, Charles Homer. *The Normans in European History.* New York: Frederick Ungar Publishing Co., 1959.

Laing, Jennifer. *Warriors of the Dark Ages.* Phoenix Mill, United Kingdom: Sutton Publishing Limited, 2000.

Russell, Phillips. *William the Conqueror.* New York: Charles Scribner's Sons, 1933.

Slocombe, George. *William the Conqueror.* New York: G. P. Putnam's Sons, 1959.

Wood, Michael. *In Search of England.* Berkeley: University of California Press, 1999.

———. *In Search of the Dark Ages.* New York: Facts on File Publications, 1987.

On the Internet

The Battle of Hastings
http://www.faculty.de.gcsu.edu/~dvess/ids/medieval/hastings/hastings3.htm

The Battle of Hastings 1066
http://www.battle1066.com/intro.shtml

The Bayeux Tapestry
http://hastings1066.com/

BBC: William the Conqueror
http://www.bbc.co.uk/history/historic_figures/william_i_king.shtml

The Domesday Book Online
http://www.domesdaybook.co.uk/index.html

Hastings: Two Kings, One Battle, and an Abbey
http://www.timetravel-britain.com/06/July/hastings.shtml

Medieval Sourcebook: The Laws of William the Conqueror
http://www.fordham.edu/halsall/source/will1-lawsb.html

Medieval Sourcebook: Truce of God—Bishopric of Terouanne, 1063
http://www.fordham.edu/halsall/source/t-of-god.html

The Middle Ages: William the Conqueror
http://history.boisestate.edu/WESTCIV/willconq/

Secrets of the Norman Invasion
http://www.secretsofthenorman invasion.com/

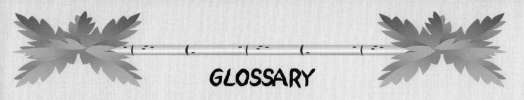

GLOSSARY

atheling (ATH-ling)—A prince.

banish (BAA-nish)—Force to leave a country or group.

battle-ax (BAA-tul aks)—An ax with a wide blade, usually used as a weapon.

cavalry (KAA-vul-ree)—Soldiers who fight from horseback.

common-law wife—A woman who is legally considered a wife after living with a man for a specified number of years, without benefit of marriage.

confiscate (KON-fih-skayt)—To take, usually by force or authority.

duress (dur-ES)—Under the influence of threat or force.

feudal (FYOO-dul)—Having to do with the political system where nobility (lords) owned the land on which their subjects (vassals) lived and worked.

fief (FEEF)—Land held by a feudal lord.

infantry (IN-fun-tree)—Foot soldiers.

javelin (JAV-lin)—A light spear.

mace—A spiky clublike weapon that can break armor.

mail—Armor made of interlinked rings of metal.

oath—A formal statement or promise.

Pict (PIKT)—An ancient tribe who lived in northern Britain.

pillage (PIL-idj)—To rob and kill, usually on a large scale.

predecessor (PREH-duh-seh-ser)—Someone who comes before.

relic (REH-lik)—A piece of the past; an object that is considered sacred because it is associated with a saint (such as the bones of a saint).

standard (STAN-derd)—A flag.

summit (SUH-mit)—The highest point.

vassal (VAA-sul)—A person granted the use of land in return for service or loyalty.

Visigoths (VIH-zih-goths)—People of ancient Europe who invaded the Roman Empire.

volley (VAH-lee)—A release of many arrows at one time.

INDEX

Abbaye-aux-Dames 27
Abbaye-aux-Hommes 27, 41
Adeliza 28, 29
Aelfgifu 29
Aethelred the Unready (King of England) 12, 16, 17, 20
Agatha 39
Alain of Brittany 21
Alexander II (Pope) 31
Alfred the Great 17, 20, 25, 30
Baldwin (Count of Flanders) 25, 26, 28
Battle Abbey 34
Bayeux Tapestry 32, 38
Canute (King of England) 16, 17
Charles the Simple (King of France) 14, 22
Domesday Book 40, 42
Edgar the Atheling (King of England) 37
Edith Swan-neck 30, 35
Edward the Confessor (King of England) 8, 16, 17, 20, 26, 28, 29, 30, 17, 31, 32, 37
Edwin (Earl of Mercia) 8, 30–31, 33, 37, 39, 40
Emma of Normandy 12, 15, 17
Falaise, France 19, 21
Fulbert 19, 20
Geoffrey (the Hammer) Martel (Count of Anjou) 22, 28
Guy, Count 28
Hardecanute (King of England) 17
Harold (Earl of Wessex; King of England) 7–10, 28–31, 32–34, 35, 37, 38, 39, 40
Harold Fairhair (King of Norway) 14
Harold Hardraade (King of Norway) 8, 10, 33, 34
Hastings, Battle of 6, 7–10, 33–34, 35, 37, 38
Henry I (son of William; King of England) 40
Henry I (King of France) 20, 22, 25, 26, 28
Herleva 19–21
Housecarls 6, 8, 33
Julius Caesar 13
Lanfranc 25, 26, 27, 31, 40
Leo IX (Pope) 26, 27

Malcolm of Scotland (King of Scotland) 39–40
Matilda of Flanders 25, 26, 27, 28, 32, 38, 39, 40
Morcar (Earl of Northumbria) 8, 9, 31, 33, 37, 40
Mortemer, Battle of 28
Nicholas II (Pope) 27
Odo 9, 10, 20, 22, 38
Peace of God 23
Ralph of Wacey 21
relics 23, 29, 30, 33, 34
Richard II (Duke of Normandy) 12, 19, 26
Richard III (Duke of Normandy) 19
Robert Fitz Wymarc 8
Robert of Mortain 10
Robert the Devil (Duke of Normandy) 18, 19–21, 23
Robert the Pious (King of France) 19
Rollo the Granger (Duke of Normandy) 14, 15, 16, 19, 22, 25
Stamford Bridge, Battle of 8, 33–34
Svein Forkbeard (King of Denmark) 17
Taillefer 10
Tostig 30, 31, 32, 33–34
Tower of London 37
Truce of God 23
Vikings 7, 12, 14, 16, 17
Wace (poet) 8, 11, 20, 21
William (Duke of Normandy, King of England)
  birth of 19, 20, 21, 22, 25
  childhood of 20–22
  death of 40
  as duke of Normandy 6, 7–10, 11, 20, 21–22, 25–34
  family tree of 14, 19
  as king of England 10, 36, 37–41, 42
  marriage of 27
  is named heir (he believes) 9, 20, 26, 30
  personality of 24, 25
William Busac of Eu 22
William of Arques 22
Witan 17, 26, 31, 37